THE WITCHES OF SCOTLAND

BY

ELIZA LYNN LINTON

British Library Cataloguing-in-Publication Data
A catalogue record for this book is available from the
British Library

CONTENTS

ELIZA LYNN LINTON 1

THE WITCHES OF SCOTLAND 3

THE DEVIL'S SECRETARY 11

ELSPETH CURSETTER AND HER FRIENDS..........17

SANDIE AND THE DEVIL 22

THE DEVIL OF GLENLUCE 26

WITCH SPIRITS 49

THE LAST OF THE WITCHES...................................54

ELIZA LYNN LINTON

Eliza Lynn Linton was born Elizabeth Lynn in Keswick, England in 1822. Her mother died when she was still in infancy, and she was brought up by her strict and devoutly religious father. After publishing a number of poems in *Ainsworth's Magazine*, the 23-year-old Lynn moved to London with a view to becoming a full-time writer. Her first two novels, *Azeth, The Egyptian* (1847) and *Amyone: A Romance in the Days of Pericles* (1848) were moderately well-received, but brought her little commercial success. In 1848, Lynn joined the staff of *The Morning Chronicle* and *All the Year Round*; in the process becoming the first woman journalist in England to draw a salary.

In 1851, Lynn published her third novel, *Realities*, a radical critique of Victorian society which was considered shocking by readers. The reaction led her to take a fourteen-year hiatus from writing fiction, and it wasn't until after her separation from her husband, W. J. Linton, that she finally attained wide popularity with her most successful works *The True History of Joshua Davidson* (1872 and *Patricia Kemball* (1874). Around this time, Linton also became well-known for her columns in the *Saturday Review*, in which she revealed herself to be a staunch right-winger, attacking – amongst other things –

the "shrieking sisterhood" of suffragettes. Her most famous essay, 'The Girl of the Period', denounced young women for the twin evils of flirting and wearing makeup.

Eliza moved to Malvern in 1895, and she died of pneumonia in 1898, during a visit to London. Although recent critical attention has gone some way towards reestablishing Linton's reputation as a novelist, it is for her reactionary journalism that she remains best-remembered.

THE WITCHES OF SCOTLAND

Mrs E. Lynn Linton

Scotland was always foremost in superstition. Her wild hills and lonely fells seemed the fit haunting-places for all mysterious powers; and long after spirits had fled, and ghosts had been laid in the level plains of the South, they were to be found lingering about the glens and glades of Scotland. Very little of graceful fancy lighted up the gloom of those popular superstitions. Even Elfame, or Faërie, was a place of dread and anguish, where the devil ruled heavy-handed and Hell claimed its yearly tithe, rather than the home of fun and beauty and petulant gaiety as with other nations: and the beautiful White Ladies, like the German Elle-women, had more of bale than bliss as their portion to scatter among the sons of men. Spirits like the goblin Gilpin Horner, full of malice and unholy cunning,—like grewsome brownies, at times unutterably terrific, at times grotesque and rude, but then more satyr-like than elfish,—like May Moulachs, lean and hairy-armed, watching over the fortunes of a family, but prophetic only of woe, not of well,—like the cruel Kelpie, hiding behind the river sedges to rush out on unwary passers-by, and strangle them beneath the waters,—like the unsained laidly*͟ Elf, who came tempting Christian women, to their souls' eternal perdition if they yielded to the desires of their bodies,—like the fatal Banshee, harbinger of death and ruin,—were the popular forms of the Scottish spirit-world; and in none of them do we find either love or gentleness, but only fierceness and crime, enmity to man and rebellion to God. But saddest and darkest and unholiest of all was the belief in witchcraft, which infested society for centuries like a sore eating through to the very heart of humanity, and which was nowhere more bitter and destructive than among the godly children of our Northern sister. Strange that the land of the Lord should have been the favourite camping-ground of Satan, that the hill of Zion should have had its roots in the depths of Tophet!

The formulas of the faith were as gloomy as the persons. The power of the evil eye; the faculty of second sight, which always saw the hearse plumes, and never the bridal roses; the supremacy of the devil in this God-governed world of ours, and the actual and practical covenant into which men and women daily entered with him; the unlimited influence of the curse, and the sin and mischief to be wrought by charm and spell; the power of casting sickness on whomsoever one would, and the ease with which a blight could be sent on the corn, and a murrain to the beasts, by those who had not wherewithal to stay their hunger for a day, these were the chief signs of that fatal power with which Satan endowed his chosen ones—those silly, luckless chapmen who bartered away their immortal souls for no mess of pottage even, and no earthly good to breath or body, but only that they might harm their neighbours and revenge themselves on those who crossed them. Sometimes, indeed, they had no need to chaffer with the devil for such faculties: as in the matter of the evil eye; for Kirk, of Aberfoyle, tells us that "some are of so venomous a Constitution, by being radiated in Envy and Malice, that they pierce and kill (like a Cockatrice) whatever Creature they first set their Eyes on in the Morning: so was it with Walter G ahame, some Time living in the Parock wherein now I am, who killed his own Cow after commending its Fatness, and shot a Hair with his Eyes, having praised its Swiftness (such was the Infection of ane Evill Eye); albeit this was unusual, yet he saw no Object but what was obvious to other Men as well as to himselfe." And a certain woman looking over the door of a byre or cowhouse, where a neighbour sat milking, shot the calf dead and dried up and sickened the cow, "by the venomous glance of her evill eye." But perhaps she had got that venom by covenant with the devil; for this was one of the prescriptive possessions of a witch, and ever the first dole from the Satanic treasury. When Janet Irving was brought to trial (1616) for unholy dealings with the foul fiend, it was proved—for was it not sworn to? and that was quite sufficient legal proof in all witchcraft cases—that he had told her "ye schoe bure ill-will to onie bodie, to look on them with opin eyis, and pray evill for thame in his name, and schoe sould get hir hartis desyre;" and in almost every witch trial in Scotland the "evil eye" formed part of the counts of indictment against the accused. The curse was as efficacious. Did a foul-mouthed old dame give a neighbour a handful of words more forcible than courteous, and did terror, or revenge, induce, or simulate, a nervous seizure in consequence, the old dame was at once carried off to the lock-up, and but few chances of escape lay between her and the stake beyond. To be skilful in healing, too, was just as dangerous as to be powerful in sickening; and to the godly and unclean of the period all sorts of devilish cantrips lay in "south-running waters" and herb drinks, and salves made of simples; while the use of bored stones, of prayers said thrice or backwards, of "mwildis" powders, or any other more patent form of witchcraft, though it might restore the sick to health, yet was fatally sure to land the user thereof at the foot of the gallows, and the testimony of the healed friend was the strongest strand in the hangman's cord. This, indeed, was the saddest feature in the whole matter—the total want of all gratitude, reliance, trustiness, or affection between a "witch" and her friends. The dearest intimate she had gave evidence against her frankly, and without a second thought of the long years of mutual help and kindliness that had gone before; the neighbour whom she had nursed night and day with all imaginable tenderness and self-devotion, if he took a craze and dreamed of witchcraft, came forward to distort and exaggerate every remedy she had used, and every art she had employed; her very children turned against her without pity or remorse, and little lips, scarce dry from the milk of her own breasts, lisped out the glibbest lies of all. Most pitiful, most sad, was the state of these poor wretches; but instructive to us, as evidencing the strength of superstition, and the weakness of every human virtue when brought into contact and collision with it. What other gifts and powers belonged to the witches will be best gathered from the stories themselves; for varied as they are, there is a strange thread of likeness running through them all; specially is there a likeness in all of a time or district, as might be expected in a matter which belonged so much to mere imitation.

Scotland played an unenviable part in the great witch panic that swept like an epidemic over Europe during the sixteenth and seventeenth centuries. It suited with the stern, uncompromising, Puritan temper, to tear this accursed thing from the heart of the nation, and offer it, bleeding and palpitating, as a sacrifice to the Lord; and accordingly we find the witch trials of Scotland conducted with more severity than elsewhere, and with a more gloomy and savage fanaticism of faith. Those who dared question the truth of even the most unreliable witnesses and the most monstrous statements were accused of atheism and infidelity—they were Sadducees and sinners—men given over to corruption and uncleanness, with whom no righteous servant could hold any terms. And then the ministers mingled themselves in the fray; and the Kirk like the Church, the presbyter like the priest, proved to be on the side of intolerance and superstition, where, unfortunately, priests of all creeds have ever been. And when James VI came with his narrow brain and selfish heart, to formularize the witch-lie into a distinct canon of arbitrary faith, and give it increased political significance and social power, the reign of humanity and common sense was at an end, and the autocracy of cruelty and superstition began. It is a dreary page in human history; but so long as a spark of superstition lingers in the world it will have its special and direct uses.

The first time we hear of Scottish witches was when St Patrick offended them and the devil alike by his uncompromising rigour against them: so they tore off a piece of a rock as he was crossing the sea and hurled it after him; which rock became the fortress of Dumbarton in the days which knew not St Patrick. Then there was the story of King Duff (968), who pined away in mortal sickness, by reason of the waxen image which had been made to destroy him; but by the fortunate discovery of a young maiden who could not bear torture silently, he was enabled to find the witches—whom he burnt at Forres in Murray, the mother of the poor maiden who could not bear torture among them: enabled, too, to save himself by breaking the wasting waxen image roasting at the "soft" fire, when almost at its last turn. Then we come to Thomas of Ercildoune, whom the Queen of Faërie loved and kept; and then to Sir Michael Scot of Balweary, that famous wizard, second to none in power; while a little further removed from those legendary times we see the dark figure of William Lord Soulis, who was boiled to death at Nine Stane Brig, in fitting punishment for his crimes. And then in 1479 twelve mean women and several wizards were burnt at Edinburgh for roasting the king in wax, and so endangering the life of the sovereign liege in a manner which no human aid could remedy; and the Earl of Mar was at their head, and very properly burnt too. And in 1480 Incubi and Succubi held the land between them, and even the young lady of Mar gave herself up to the embraces of an Incubus—a hideous monster, utterly loathsome and deadly to behold; and if the young ladies of the nobility could do such things, what might not be expected from the commonalty? But now we come out into the light of written history, and the story of "The Devil's Secretary."

THE DEVIL'S SECRETARY

On the 26th of December, 1590, John Fian, *alias* Cuningham* 'spelt Johanne Feane, *alias* Cwninghame), master of the school at Saltpans, Lothian, and contemptuously recorded as "Secretar and Register to the Devil," was arraigned for witchcraft and high treason. There were twenty counts against him, the least of which would have been enough to have lighted up a witch-fire on that fatal Castle Hill, for the bravest and best in the land. First, he was accused of entering into a covenant with Satan, who appeared to him in white, as he lay in bed, musing and thinking ("mwsand and pansand," says the dittay in its quaint language) how he should be revenged on Thomas Trumbill, for not having whitewashed his room, according to agreement. After promising his Satanic majesty allegiance and homage, he received his mark, which later was found under his tongue, with two pins therein thrust up to their heads. Again, he was found guilty—"fylit" is the old legal term—of "feigning himself to be sick in the said Thomas Trumbill's chamber, where he was stricken in great ecstacies and trances, lying by the space of two or three hours dead, his spirit taken, and suffered himself to be carried and transported to many mountains, as he thought through all the world, according to his depositions." Note, that these depositions were made in the midst of fearful torture, and recanted the instant after. Also, he was found guilty of suffering himself to be carried to North Berwick church, where, together with many others, he did homage to Satan, as he stood in the pulpit, making doubtful speeches, saying, "Many come to the fair, and all buy not wares;" and desired him "not to fear though he was grim, for he had many servants who should never want, or ail nothing, so long as their hair was on, and should never let one tear fall from their eyes so long as they served him;" and he gave them lessons, and said, "Spare not to do evil, and to eat and drink and be blithe, taking rest and ease, for he should raise them up at the latter day gloriously." But the pith of the indictment was that he, Fian, and sundry others to be spoken of hereafter, entered into a league with Satan to wreck the king on his way to Denmark, whither, in a fit of clumsy gallantry, he had set out to visit his future queen. While he was sailing to Denmark, Fian and a whole crew of witches and wizards met Satan at sea, and the master, giving an enchanted cat into Robert Grierson's hand, bade him "cast the same into the sea, holà," which was accordingly done; and a pretty capful of wind the consequence. Then, when the king was returning from Denmark, the devil promised to raise a mist which should wreck him on English ground. To perform which feat he took something like a football—it seemed to Dr. Fian like a wisp—and cast it into the sea, whereupon arose the great mist which nearly drove the cumbrous old pedant on to English ground, where our strong-fisted queen would have made him pay for his footing in a manner not quite congenial to his tastes. But, being a Man of God, none of these charms and devilries prevailed against him. A further count was, that once again he consorted with Satan and his crew, still in North Berwick church, where they paced round the church wider shins (wider scheins?), that is, contrary to the way of the sun. Fian blew into the lock—a favourite trick of his—to open the door, and blew in the lights which burned blue, and were like big black candles held in an old man's hand round about the pulpit. Here Satan as a "mekill blak man, with ane blak baird stikand out lyke ane gettis (goat's) baird; and ane hie ribbit neise, falland doun scharp lyke the beik of ane halk; with ane lang rumpill (tail); cled in ane blak tatie goune, and ane ewill favorit scull bonnett on his heid; haifand ane blak buik in his hand," preached to them, commanding them to be good servants to him, and he would be a good master to them, and never let them want. But he made them all very angry by calling Robert Grierson by his Christian name. He ought to have been called "Ro" the Comptroller, or "Rob the Rower." This slip of the master's displeased them sorely, and they ran "hirdie girdie" in great excitement, for it was against all etiquette to be named by their earthly names; indeed, they always received new names when the devil gave them their infernal christening, and they made themselves over to him and denied their holy baptism. It was at this meeting that John Fian was specially accused of rifling the graves of the dead, and dismembering their bodies for charms. And many other things did this Secretar and Register to the devil. Once, at the house of David Seaton's mother, he breathed into the hand of a woman sitting by the fire, and opened a lock at the other end of the kitchen. Once he raised up four candles on his horse's two ears, and a fifth on the staff which a man riding with him carried in his hand. These magic candles gave as much light as the sun at noonday, and the man was so terrified that he fell dead on his own threshold. He sent an evil spirit, who tormented a man for twenty weeks; and he was seen to chase a cat, and in the chase to be carried so high over a hedge that he could not touch her head. The dittay says he flew through the air—a not infrequent mode of progression with such people. When asked why he hunted the cat, he said that Satan had need of her, and that he wanted all the cats he could lay hands on, to cast into the sea, and cause storms and shipwrecks. He was further accused of endeavouring to bewitch a young maiden by his devilish cantrips* and horrid charms, but by a wile of the girl's mother, up to men's arts, he practised on a heifer's hairs instead of the girl's, and the result was that a luckless young cow went lowing after him everywhere—even into his school-room—rubbing herself against him, and exhibiting all the languish and desire of a love-sick young lady. A curious old plate represents John Fian and the heifer in grotesque attitudes; the heifer with large, drooping, amorous eyes, intensely ridiculous—the schoolmaster with his magic wand drawing circles in the sand. These, with divers smaller charges, such as casting horoscopes, and wearing modewart's (mole's) feet upon him, amounting in all to twenty counts, formed the sum of the indictment against him. He was put to the torture. First, his head was "thrawed* with a rope" for about an hour, but still he would not confess; then they tried fair words and coaxed him, but with no better success; and then they put him to the "most severe and cruell pains in the worlde," namely, the boots, till his legs were completely crushed, and the blood and marrow spouted out. After the third stroke he became speechless; and they, supposing it to be the devil's mark which kept him silent, searched for that mark, that by its discovery the spell might be broken. So they found it, as stated before, under his tongue, with two charmed pins stuck up to their heads therein. When they were drawn out—that is, after some further torture—he confessed anything which it pleased his tormentors to demand of him, saying how, just now, the devil had been to

15

him all in black, but with a white wand in his hand; and how, on his, Fian's, renouncing him, he had broke his wand, and disappeared. The next day he recanted this confession. He was then somewhat restored to himself, and had mastered the weakness of his agony. Whereupon it was assumed that the devil had visited him through the night, and had marked him afresh. They searched him—pulling off every nail with a turkas, or smith's pincers, and then thrusting in needles up to their heads; but finding nothing more satanic than blood and nerves, they put him to worse tortures, as a revenge. He made no other relapse, but remained constant now to the end; bearing his grievous pains with patience and fortitude, and dying as a brave man always knows how to die, whatever the occasion. Finding that nothing more could be made of him, they mercifully came to an end. He was strangled and burnt "in the Castle Hill of Edinburgh, on a Saterdaie, in the ende of Januarie last past 1591;" ending a may be loose and not over-heroic life in a manner worthy of the most glorious martyr of history. John Fian, schoolmaster of Saltpans with no great idea to support him, and no admiring friends to cheer him on, bore himself as nobly as any hero of them all, and vindicated the honour of manhood and natural strength in a way that exalts our common human nature into something godlike and divine.

ELSPETH CURSETTER AND HER FRIENDS

Elspeth Cursetter was tried, May 29, 1602, for all sorts of bad actions. She bade one of her victims "get the bones of ane tequhyt (linnet), and carry thame in your claithes"; and she gave herself out as knowing evil, and able to do it too, when and to whomsoever she would; and she sat down before the house of a man who refused her admittance—for she was an ill-famed old witch, and every one dreaded her—saying "Ill might they all thrive, and ill may they speed," whereby in fourteen days' time the man's horse fell just where she had sat, and was killed most lamentably. But she cured a neighbour's cow by drawing a cog of water out of the burn that ran before William Anderson's door, coming back and taking three straws—one for William Anderson's wife, and one for William Coitt's wife, and one for William Bichen's wife—which she threw into the pail with the water, then put the same on the cow's back; by which charm the three straws danced in the water, and the water bubbled as it had been boiling. Then Elspeth took a little quantity of this charmed water, and thrust her arm up to the elbow into the cow's throat, and on the instant the cow rose up as well as she had ever been; but William Anderson's ox, which was on the hill, dropped down dead. Likewise she worked unholy cantrips for a sick friend with a paddock (toad), in the mouth of a pail of water, which toad was too large to get down the mouth, and when it was cast forth another man sickened and died immediately: and she spake dangerous words to a child, saying, "Wally fall that quhyt head of thine, but the pox will tak the away frae thy mother." As it proved, for the little white head was laid low a short time after, when the small-pox raged through the land. "Thow can tell eneough yf thow lyke," said the mother to her afterwards, "that could tell that my bairne wold die so long befoir the tyme." "I can tell eneugh if I durst," replied Elspeth, over proud of her safety. But in spite of all this testimony, Elspeth got off with "arbitrary punishment," which did not include burning or strangling, so was luckier than her neighbours. Luckier than poor Jonet Rendall was, who, on the nth of November (1629), was proved a witch by the bleeding of the corpse of the poor wretch whom she had "enchanted" to his death. For "as soon as she came in the corpse having lain a good space, and not having bled any, immediately bled much blood, as a sure token that she was the author of his death." And had she not said, too, when a certain man refused her a Christmas lodging, "that it wald be weill if the gude man of that hous sould make ane other yule banket" (Christmas banquet); by which curse had he not died in fifteen days after? Wherefore was she a proved murderess as well as witch, and received the doom appointed to both alike. Alexander Drummond was a warlock who cured all kinds of horrid diseases, the very names of which are enough to make one ill; and he had a familiar, which had attended him for "neir this fifty yeiris:" so he was convicted and burnt.

Then came Jonet Forsyth, great in her art. She could cast sickness on any one at sea, and cure him again by a salt-water bath; she could transfer any disease from man to beast, so that when the beast died and was opened, nothing could be found where its heart should have been but "a blob of water;" she knew how to charm and sain* all kinds of cattle by taking three drops of a beastie's blood on All Hallow E'en, and sprinkling the same in the fire within the innermost chamber; she went at seed time and bewitched a stack of barley belonging to Michael Reid, so that for many years he could never make it into wholesome malt; and this she did for the gain of Robert Reid, changing the "profit" of the grain backwards and forwards between the two, according as they challenged or displeased her. All this did Jonet Forsyth of Birsay, to the terror of her neighbours and the ultimate ruin of herself, both in soul and body. Then came Catherine Oswald, spouse to Robert Aitcheson, in Niddrie, who was brought to trial for being "habite and repute" a witch—defamed by Elizabeth Toppock herself a witch and, as is so often the case, a dear friend of Katie's. Elizabeth need not have been so eager to get rid of her dear friend and gossip,

19

for she was burnt afterwards for the same crimes as those for which poor Catherine suffered the halter and the stake. It seems that Katie was bad for her enemies. She was offended at Adam Fairbairn and his wife, so she made their "twa kye run mad and rammish‡ to died," and also made a gentleman's bairn that they had a-fostering run wood (mad) and die. And she fired William Heriot's kiln, full of grain; and burnt all his goods before his eyes; and made his wife, in a "frantick humour," drown herself; and she cursed John Clark's ground, so that for four years after "by hir sorceries, naether kaill, lint, hempe, nor any other graine" would grow thereon, though doubly "laboured and sowen." She bewitched Thomas Scott by telling him that he looked as well as when Bessie Dobie was living, whereby he immediately fell so deadly sick that he could not proceed further, but was carried on a horse to Newbiggin, where he lay until the morrow, when "a wife" came in and told him he was forespoken. And other things as mischievous—and as true—did Catherine Oswald, as the Record testifies. She was well defended, and might have got off, but that a witness deposed to having seen Mr John Aird the minister, and a most zealous witch-finder, prick her in the shoulder with a pin, and that no blood followed thereafter, nor did she shrink as with pain or feeling. And as there was no gainsaying the evidence of the witch-mark, Satan and Mr John Aird claimed their own. Was Catherine's brand like a "blew spot, or a little tate, or reid spots, like flea-biting?" or with "the fleshsunk in and hallow?" according to the description of such places, published by Mr John Bell, minister of the gospel in Gladsmuir. We are seldom told of what precise character the marks were, only that they were found, pricked, and tested, and the witch hung or burnt on their testimony.

SANDIE AND THE DEVIL

Soon after Catherine Oswald's execution, one of her crew or coven, who had been with her on the great storm in "the borrowing days (in anno 1625), on the Brae of the Saltpans," a noted warlock, by name Alexander Hunter, or Hamilton, *alias* Hatteraick, which last name he had gotten from the devil, was brought to execution on the Castle Hill. It was in 1629 that he was taken. It was proved that on Kingston hills he had met with the devil as a black man, or, as Sinclair says, as a mediciner; and often afterwards he would meet him riding on a black horse, or he would appear as a corbie, cat, or dog. When Alexander wanted him he would beat the ground with a fir stick lustily, crying, "Rise up, foul thief!" for the master got but hard names at times from his servants. This fir stick, and four shillings sterling, the devil gave to him when the compact was first made between them; and he confessed, moreover, that when raised in this manner he could only be got rid of by sacrificing to him a cat or dog, or such like, "quick." Also he set on fire Provost Cockburn's mill of corn, by taking three stalks from his stacks, and burning them on Garleton Hills; and he owned to a deadly hatred against Lady Ormiston, because she once refused him "ane almous," and called him "ane custroune carle." So, to punish her, he and some witches raised the devil in Salton

Wood, where he appeared like a man in gray clothes, and gave him the bottom of a blue clew, telling him to lay it at the lady's door: "which he and the women having done, 'the lady and her daughter were soon thereafter bereft of their naturall lyfe.' " But Sinclair's account is the most graphic. I will give it in his own words:—

"Anent Hattaraick, an old Warlock.

"This man's name was Sandie Hunter, who called himself Sandie Hamilton, and it seems so called Hattaraik by the devil, and so by others as a Nickname. He was first a Neatherd in East Lothian, to a gentleman there. He was much given to charming and cureing of men and Beasts, by words and spels. His charms sometimes succeeded and sometimes not. On a day, herding his kine upon a Hill side in the summer time, the Devil came to him in form of a Mediciner, and said, 'Sandie, you have too long followed my trade, and never acknowledged me for your master. You must not take on with me, and I will make you more perfect in your calling. Whereupon the man gave up himself to the devil and received his Mark with this new name. After this he grew very famous throw the countrey for his charming cureing of diseases in men and beasts, and turned a vagrant fellow like a Jockie, gaining Meat, Flesh, and Money by his Charms, such was the ignorance of many at that time.

"Whatever House he came to, none durst refuse Hattaraik

any alms, rather for his ill than his good. One day he came to the yait of Samuelstown, when some Friends after dinner were going to Horse. A young Gentleman, Brother to the Lady, seeing him, switcht him about the ears, saying, 'You Warlok Cairle, what have you to do here?' whereupon the Fellow goes away grumbling, and was overheard to say, 'You shall dear buy this, ere it be long.' This was *Damnum Minatum.* The young Gentleman conveyed his Friends a far way off, and came home that way again, where he slept. After supper, taking his horse and crossing Tine-water to go home, he rides throw a shadowy piece of a Haugh, commonly called the Allers, and the evening being somewhat dark he met with some Persons there that begat a dreadful consternation in him, which for the most part he would never reveal. This was *malum secutum.* When he came home, the Servants observed terror and fear in his countenance. The next day he became distracted, and was bound for several days. His sister, the Lady Samuelstoun, hearing of it, was heard to say, 'Surely that knave Hattaraik is the cause of his Trouble. Call for him in all haste.' When he had come to her, 'Sandie,' says she, 'what is this you have done to my brother William?' 'I told him,' says he, 'I should make him repent his striking of me at the Yait lately.' She gave the Rogue fair words, and promising him his Pock full of Meal with Beef and Cheese, persuaded the Fellow to cure him again. He undertook the business;

'but I must first,' says he, 'have one of his Sarks,' which was soon gotten. What pranks he plaid with it cannot be known. But within a short while the gentleman recovered his health. When Hatteraik came to receive his wages, he told the Lady, 'Your Brother William shal quickly goe off the Countrey but shall never return.' She, knowing the Fellow's prophecies to hold true, caused her Brother to make a Disposition to her of all his patrimony, to the defrauding of his younger brother George. After that this Warlock had abused the Countrey for a long time, he was at last apprehended at Dunbar, and brought into Edinburgh, and burnt upon the Castle Hill. But not until he had delated several others of hitherto good repute, so that for the next few months the witchfinder's hands were full."

One of the most extraordinary tales I have to relate was
that wonderful bit of knavery and credulity called

THE DEVIL OF GLENLUCE

when Master Tom Campbell set the whole country in a
flame, and brought no end of notice and sympathy upon his
house and family. In 1654 one Gilbert Campbell was a weaver
in Glenluce, a small village not far from Newton Stewart.
Tom, his eldest son, and the most important personage in
the drama, was a student at Glasgow College; and there was
a certain old blaspheming beggar, called Andrew Agnew—
afterwards hanged at Dumfries for his atheism, having said,
in the hearing of credible witnesses, that "there was no God
but salt, meal, and water"—who every now and then came
to Glenluce to ask alms. One day old Andrew visited the
Campbells as usual, but got nothing; at which he cursed
and swore roundly, and forthwith sent a devil to haunt the
house, for it was soon after this refusal that the stirs began,
and the connection was too apparent to be denied. For what
could they be but the malice of the devil sent by old Andrew
in revenge? Young Tom Campbell was the worst beset of all,
the demon perpetually whistling and rioting about him, and
playing him all sorts of diabolical and malevolent tricks.
Once, too, Jennet, the young daughter, going to the well,

heard a whistling behind her like that produced by "the small slender glass whistles of children," and a voice like the damsel's, saying, "I'll cast thee, Jennet, into the well! I'll cast thee, Jennet, into the well!" About the middle of November, when the days were dark and the nights long, things got very bad. The foul fiend threw stones in at the doors and windows, and down the chimney head; cut the warp and threads of Campbell's loom; slit the family coats and bonnets and hose and shoon into ribbons; pulled off the bed-clothes from the sleeping children, and left them cold and naked, besides administering sounding slaps on those parts of their little round rosy persons usually held sacred to the sacrifices of the rod; opened chests and trunks, and strewed the contents over the floor; knocked everything about, and ill-treated bairn and brother; and, in fact, persecuted the whole family in the most merciless manner. The weaver sent his children away, thinking their lives but barely safe, and *in their absence there were no assaults whatever*—a thing to be specially noted. But on the minister's representing to him that he had done a grievous sin in thus withdrawing them from God's punishments, they were brought back again in contrition. Only Tom was left behind, and nothing ensued until Tom appeared; but unlucky Tom brought back the devil with him, and then there was no more peace to be had.

On the Sunday following Master Tom's return, the house

was set on fire—the devil's doing: but the neighbours put the flames out again before much damage had ensued. Monday was spent in prayer; but on Tuesday the place was again set on fire, to be again saved by the neighbours' help. The weaver, in much trouble, went to the minister, and besought him to take back that unlucky Tom, whom the devil so cruelly followed and molested; which request he, after a time, "condescended to," though assuring the weaver that he would find himself deceived if he thought that the devil would quit with the boy. And so it proved; for Tom, having now indoctrinated some of his juniors with the same amount of mechanics and legerdemain as he himself possessed, managed that they should be still sore troubled—the demon cutting their clothes, throwing peats down the chimney, pulling off turf and "feal" from the roof and walls, stealing their coats, pricking their poor bodies with pins, and raising such a clamour that there was no peace or rest to be had.

The case was becoming serious. Glenluce objected to be made the head-quarters of the devil; and the ministers convened a solemn meeting for fast and humiliation; the upshot of which was that weaver Campbell was led to take back his unlucky Tom, with the devil or without him. For this was the point at issue in the beginning; the motive of which is not hard to be discoverd. Whereupon Tom returned; but as he crossed the threshold he heard a voice "forbidding him to enter that house, or any other place where his father's calling was exercised." Was Tom, the Glasgow student, afraid of being made a weaver, consent or none demanded? In spite of the warning voice he valiantly entered, and his persecutions began at once. Of course they did. They were tremendous, unheard of, barbarous; in fact, so bad that he was forced to return once more for a time to the minister's house; but his imitator or disciple left behind carried on business in his absence. On Monday, the 12th day of February, the demon began to speak to the family, who, nothing afraid, answered quite cheerily: so they and the devil had long confidential chats together, to the great improvement of mind and morals. The ministers, hearing of this, convened again, and met at weaver Campbell's to see what they could do. As soon as they entered, Satan began: "Quum literatum is good Latin," quoth he. These were the first words of the Latin rudiments, as taught in the grammar-school. Tom's classical knowledge was coming into play.

After a while he cried out, "A dog! a dog!" The minister, thinking he was alluded to, answered, "He thought it no evil to be reviled of him;" to which Satan replied civilly, "It was not you, sir, I spoke to: I meant the dog there;" for there was a dog standing behind backs. They then went to prayer, during which time Tom—or the devil—remained reverently silent; his education being not yet carried out to the point of scoffing. Immediately after prayer was ended, a counterfeit voice cried out, "Would you know the witches of Glenluce? I will tell of them," naming four of five persons of indifferent repute, but one of whom was dead. The weaver told the devil this, thinking to have caught him tripping; but the foul fiend answered promptly, "It is true she is dead long ago, but her spirit is living with us in the world."

The minister replied, saying, "Though it was not convenient to speak to such an excommunicated and intercommuned person, 'the Lord rebuke thee, Satan, and put thee to silence. We are not to receive information from thee, whatsoever fame any person goes under. Thou art seeking but to seduce this family, for Satan's kingdom is not divided against itself.'" After which little sparring there was prayer again; so Tom did not take much by this move.

All the while the young Glasgow student was very hardly holden, so that there was more prayer on his special behalf. The devil then said, on their rising, "Give me a spade and a shovel, and depart from the house for seven days, and I will make a grave and lie down in it, and shall trouble you no more."

The good man Campbell answered, "Not so much as a straw shall be given thee, through God's assistance, even though that would do it. God shall remove thee in due time." Satan cried out, impudently, "I shall not remove for you. I have my commission from Christ to tarry and vex this family." Says the minister, coming to the weaver's assistance, "A permission thou hast, indeed; but God will stop it in due time." Says the demon, respectfully, "I have, sir, a commission which perhaps will last longer than yours." And the minister died in the December of that year, says Sinclair. Furthermore, the demon said he had given Tom his commission to keep. Interrogated, that young gentleman replied in an off-hand way, that "he had had something put into his pocket, but it did not tarry." They then began to search about for the foul fiend, and one gentleman said, "We think this voice speaks out of the children." The foul fiend, very angry at this—or Master Tom frightened—cries out, "You lie! God shall judge you for your lying; and I and my father will come and fetch you to hell with warlock thieves." So the devil discharged (forbade) the gentleman to speak anything, saying, "Let him that hath a commission speak (meaning the minister), for he is the servant of God." The minister then had a little religious controversy with the devil, who answered at last, simply, "I knew not these scriptures till my father taught me them." Nothing of all this disturbing the easy faith of the audience, they, through the minister, whom alone he would obey, conjured him to tell them who he was; whereupon he said that he was an evil spirit come from the bottomless pit of hell, to vex this house, and that Satan was his father. And then there appeared a naked hand, and an arm from the elbow downward, beating on the floor till the house did shake again, and a loud and fearful crying, "Come up, father! come up, father! I will send my father among ye! See! there he is behind your backs!"

Says the minister, "I saw, indeed, a hand and an arm, when the stroke was given and heard."

Says the devil, "Saw ye that? It was not my hand, it was my father's; my hand is more black in the loof."

"Oh!" said Gilbert Campbell, in an ecstacy, "that I might see thee as well as I hear thee!"

"Would ye see me?" says the foul thief. "Put out the candle, and I shall come but* the house among you like fire-balls; I shall let ye see me indeed."

Alexander Bailie of Dunraget said to the minister, "Let us go ben,‡ and see if there is any hand to be seen." But the demon exclaimed, "No! let him (the minister) come ben alone: he is a good honest man: his single word may be believed." He then abused Mr. Robert Hay, a very honest gentleman, very ill with his tongue, calling him witch and warlock: and a little while after, cried out, "A witch! a witch! there's a witch sitting upon the ruist! take her away." He meant that there was a hen sitting on one of the rafters. They then went to prayer again, and, when ended, the devil cried out, "If the good man's son's prayers at the College of Glasgow did not prevail with God, my father and I had wrought a mischief here ere now." Ah, Master Tom, did you then know so much of prayer and the inclining of the counsels of God?

Alexander Bailie said, "Well, I see you acknowledge a God, and that prayer prevails with him, and therefore we must pray to God, and commit the event to him." To whom the devil replied, having an evident spite against Alexander Bailie, "Yea, sir, you speak of prayer, with your broad-lipped hat" (for the gentleman had lately gotten a hat in the fashion with broad lips); "I'll bring a pair of shears from my father's which shall clip the lips of it a little." And Alexander Bailie presently heard a pair of shears go clipping round his hat, "which he lifted, to see if the foul thief had meddled with it."

Then the fiend fell to prophesying. "Tom was to be a merchant, Bob a smith, John a minister, and Hugh a lawyer," all of which came to pass. Turning to Jennet, the good man's daughter, he cried, "Jennet Campbell, Jennet Campbell, wilt thou cast me thy belt?"

Quoth she, "What a widdy would thou do with my belt?"

"I would fain," says he, "fasten my loose bones together."

A younger daughter was sitting "busking her puppies"

(dressing her puppets, dolls), as young girls are used to do. He threatens to "ding out her harns," that is, to brain her; but says she quietly, "No, if God be to the fore," and so falls to her work again. The good wife having brought out some bread, was breaking it, so that every one of the company should have a piece. Cries he, "Grissel Wyllie! Grissel Wyllie! give me a piece of that haver bread.*_ I have gotten nothing this day but a bit from Marritt," that is, as they speak in the country, Margaret. The minister said to them all, "Beware of that! for it is sacrificing to the devil!" Marritt was then called, and inquired if she had given the foul fiend any of her haver bread. "No," says she; "but when I was eating my due piece this morning, something came and clicked it out of my hands."

The evening had now come, and the company prepared to depart; the minister, and the minister's wife, Alexander Bailie of Dunraget, with his broad-lipped hat, and the rest. But the devil cried out in a kind of agony—

"Let not the minister go! I shall burn the house if he goes." Weaver Campbell, desperately frightened, besought the minister to stay; and he, not willing to see them come to mischief, at last consented. As he turned back into the house, the devil gave a great gaff of laughing, saying, "Now, sir! you have done my bidding!" which was unhandsome of Tom—very.

Four distinguished Victorian witchcraft writers: Mrs E. Lynn Linton, Lady Lucie Duff-Gordon, Amelia Edwards, Pauline Bradford Mackie

Dr Fian and his coven at North Berwick. See the story entitled "The Devil's Secretary" by Mrs Lynn Linton

A nineteenth-century illustration of a witches' coven. Note the devil figure at the rear providing the music for the ritual dance

"Not thine, but in obedience to God, have I returned to bear this man company whom thou dost afflict," says the minister, nowise discomposed, and not disdaining to argue matters clearly with the devil.

Then the minister "discharged" all from speaking to the demon, saying, "that when it spoke to them they must only kneel and pray to God." This did not suit the demon at all. He roared mightily, and cried, "What! will ye not speak to me? I shall strike the bairns, and do all manner of mischief!" No answer was returned; and again the children were slapped and beaten on their rosy parts—where children are accustomed to be whipped. After a while this ended too, and then the fiend called out to the good-wife, "Grissel, put out the candle!"

"Shall I do it?" says she to the minister's wife.

"No," says that discreet person, "for then you shall obey the devil."

Upon which the devil shouted, with a louder voice, "Put out the candle!" No one obeyed, and the candle continued burning. "Put out the candle, I say!" cries he, more terribly than before. Grissel, not caring to continue the uproar, put it out. "And now," says he, "I will trouble you no more this night." For by this time I should suppose that Master Tom was sleepy, and tired, and hoarse.

Once again the ministers and gentlemen met for prayer

and exorcism; when it is to be presumed that Tom was not with them, for everything was quiet; but soon after the stirs began again, and Tom and the rest were sore molested. Gilbert Campbell made an appeal to the Synod of Presbyters, a committee of whom appointed a special day of humiliation in February, 1656, for the freeing of the weaver's house from this affliction. In consequence whereof, from April to August, the devil was perfectly quiet, and the family lived together in peace. But after this the mischief broke out again afresh. Perhaps Tom had come home from college, or his father had renewed his talk of settling him firmly to his own trade: whatever the cause, the effect was certain, the devil had come back to Glenluce.

One day, as the good-wife was standing by the fire, making the porridge for the children, the demon came and snatched the "tree-plate," on which was the oat-meal, out of her hand, and spilt all the meal. "Let me have the tree-plate again," says Grissel Wyllie, very humbly; and it came flying back to her. "It is like if she had sought the meal too she might have got it, such is his civility when he is entreated," says Sinclair. But this would have been rather beyond even Master Tom's power of legerdemain. Things after this went very ill. The children were daily thrashed with heavy staves, and every one in the family underwent much personal damage; until, as a climax, on the eighteenth of September, the demon said he would burn the house down, and did, in fact, set it on fire. But it was put out again, before much damage was done.

After a time—probably by Tom's going away, or becoming afraid of being found out—the devil was quieted and laid for ever; and Master Tom employed his intellect and energies in other ways than terrifying his father's family to death, and making stirs which went by the name of demoniac.

This account is taken almost verbatim from an article of mine in "All the Year Round;" and if a larger space has been given to this than to many other stories, it is because there was more colouring, and more distinctness in the drawing, than in anything else that I have read. Though scarcely belonging to a book on witches, there is yet a hook and eye, if a very slender one, in the fact that the old beggar, Andrew Agnew, was hanged; and we may be sure that it was not only his atheism, but also his naughty tricks with Satan, and his connection with the devil of Glenluce, that helped to fit the hangman's rope round his neck. There are many other stories of haunted houses, notably, Mr Monpesson's at Tedworth caused by the Demon Drummer, and the Woodstock Devil who harried the Parliamentary Commissioners to within an inch of their lives, and others to the full as interesting; but there is no hook and eye with them—nothing by which they can be hung on to the sad string of witches, or witchcraft murders. Baxter has two or three such stories;

and the curious in such matters will find a large amount of interesting matter in the various works referred to at the foot of the pages; matter which could not be introduced here, because of its not belonging strictly to the subject in hand. I do not think that any candid or unprejudiced person will fail in seeing the dark shadow of fraud and deceit flung over every such account remaining. The importance of which, to me, is Lord, for this!" But it was not much to thank him for in general; tor the old adage seems to have been pretty nearly kept to, and the cooks, at least, not to speak of the meat, to be of the very lowest description. The poor witches never got more from the devil than what they might have had at home; which was one more added to the many proofs that the mind cannot travel beyond its own sphere of knowledge, and that even hallucinations are bounded by experience, and clairvoyance by the past actual vision.

Then Isobell went to the Downie Hills, to see the "gude wichtis" who had wrought Bessie Dunlop and Alesoun Peirsoun such sad mishap. The hill side opened and she went in. Here she got meat more than she could eat, which was a rare thing for her to do in those days, and seemed to her one of the most noticeable things of the visit. The Queen of Faërie was bravely clothed in white linen, and white and brown clothes, but she was nothing like the glorious creature who bewitched Thomas of Ercildoun with her winsom looks and golden hair; and the king was a braw man, well favoured and broad faced; just an ordinary man and woman of the better classes, buxom, brave, and comely, as Isobell Gowdie and her like would naturally take to be the ultimate perfection of humanity. But it was not all sunshine and delight even in the hill of Faërie, for there were "elf bullis rowting and skoylling" up and down, which frightened poor Isobell, as well as her auditory: for here she was interrupted and bidden on another track. She then went on to say that when they took away any cow's milk they did so by twining and platting a rope the wrong way and in the devil's name, drawing the tether in between the cow's hinder feet, and out between her fore feet. The only way to get back the milk was to cut the rope. When they took away the strength of any one's ale in favour of themselves or others, they used to take a little quantity out of each barrel, in the devil's name (they never forgot this formula), and then put it into the ale they wished to strengthen; and no one had power to keep their ale from them, save those who had well sanctified the brewing. Also she and others made a clay picture of a little child, which was to represent all the male children of the Laird of Parkis. John Taylor brought home the clay in his "plaid newk" (corner), his wife brake it very small like meal, and sifted it, and poured water in among it in the devil's name, and worked it about like rye porridge ("vrought it werie sore, lyk rye-bowt") and made it into a picture of the Laird of Parkis' son. "It haid all the pairtis and merkis of a child, such as heid, eyes, nose, handis, foot, mowth, and little lippes. It wanted no mark of a child; and the handis of it folded down by its sydes." This precious image, which was like a lump of dough or a skinned sucking pig, was put to the fire till it shrivelled and became red as a coal; they put it to the fire every other day, and by the wicked power enclosed in this charm all the male children of the Laird of Parkis would suffer, unless it were broken up. She and the rest went in and out their neighbours' houses, sometimes as jackdaws, sometimes as hares, cats, &c., and ate and drank of the best; and they took away the virtue of all things left "unsained;" and each had their own powers. "Bot," said Isobell, sorrowfully, "now I haw no power at all." In another confession she told all about her Coven. There were thirteen in each, and every person had a nickname, and a spirit to wait on her. She could not remember the names of all, but she gave what she could. Swein clothed in grass green waited on Margaret Wilson called Pickel-nearest-the-wind: Rorie in yellow waited on Bessie Wilson, or Throw-the-corn-yard: the Roaring Lion in seagreen waited on Isobell Nichol, or Bessie Rule: Mak Hector, a young-like devil, clothed in grass green, was appropriated by Jean Martin, daughter to Margaret Wilson (Pickle-nearest-the-wind), the Maiden of the Coven and called Over-the-Dyke-with-it; this name given to her because the devil always takes the maiden in his hand next him, and when he would leap they both cry out, "Over the dyke with it!" Robert the Rule in sad dun, a commander of the spirits, waited on Margaret Brodie, Thief-of-hell-wait-upon-herself: he waited also on Bessie Wilson, otherwise Throw-the-corn-yard: Isobell's own spirit was the Red Riever, and he was ever clothed in black; the eighth spirit was Robert the Jakes, aged, and clothed in dun, "ane glaiked gowked spirit," and he waited on Bessie Hay, otherwise Able-and-Stout: the ninth was Laing, serving Elspet Nishie, re-named Bessie Bauld; the tenth was Thomas, a faerie:—but there Isobell's questioners stopped her, afraid to hear aught of the "guide wychtis," who might be then among them, injuring those who offended them to death. So no more information was given of the spirits of the Coven. She then told them that to raise a wind they took a rag of cloth which they wetted, then knocked on a stone with a beetle (a flat piece of wood) saying thrice—

"I knok this ragg wpon this stane,

To raise the wind in the Divelle's name;

It sall not lye, vntil I please againe!"

When the wind was to be laid, they dried the rag, and said thrice—

"We lay the wind in the divellis name,

43

It sall not rise quhill we lyk to raise it again!"

And if the wind would not cease the instant after they said this, they called to their spirit: "Thieffe! thieffe! conjure the wind and caws it to lye!" As for elf-arrow heads, the devil shapes them with his own hand, and then delivers them to elf boys who sharpen and trim them with a thing like a packing-needle: and when Isobell was in elf-land she saw the boys sharpening and trimming them. Those who trimmed them, she said, are little ones, hollow and hump-backed, and speak gruffly like. When the devil gave the arrows to the witches he used to say—

"Shoot these in my name,

And they sall not goe heall hame."

And when the witches shoot them, which they do by "spanging" them from their thumb nails, they say—

"I shoot yon man in the devillis name,

He sall nott win heall hame!

And this salbe alswa trw,

Thair sall not be an bitt of him on liew."*

Isobell had great talent for rhymes. She told the court how, when the witches wanted to transform themselves into the shape of hare or cat, they said thrice over—always thrice—

"I sall goe intill ane haire,

With sorrow, and sych, and mickle caire;

And I sall goe in the divellis name,

Ay whill I com hom againe."

Once Isobell said this rhyme when Patrik Papley's servants were going to labour. They had their dogs with them, and the dogs hunted her—she in the form of a hare. Very hard pressed, and weary, she had just time to run to her own house, get behind the chest, and repeat—

"Hair, hair, God send thé caire,

I am in a hairis likeness now,

But I sall be a woman ewin now;

Hair, hair, God send thé caire!"

Else the dogs would have worried her, and posterity have lost her confessions. Many other doggrels did Isobell teach her judges; but they were all of the same character as those already given: scanty rhymes in the devil's name, when they were not actual paraphrases of the mass book. Some were for healing and some for striking; some in the name of God and all the saints, others in the devil's name, boldly and nakedly used; but both equally damnable in the eyes of the judges, and equally worthy of death. The elf-arrows spoken of before were of great use. The devil gave them to his coven and they shot men and women dead, right and left. Sometimes they missed, as when Isobell shot at the Laird of Park as he was crossing the burn, and missed, for which Bessie Hay gave her a great cuff: also Margaret Brodie, when she shot at Mr Harie Forbes, the minister at Auldearne, he being by the standing stanes; whereupon she asked if she should shoot again, but the devil answered, "Not! for we wold nocht get his lyf at that tym." Finding the elf-arrows useless against Mr Harie Forbes, they tried charms and incantations once when he was sick. They made a bag, into which they put the flesh, entrails, and gall of a toad, a hare's liver, barley grains, nail pairings, and bits of rag, steeping all in water, while Satan stood over them, saying—and they repeating after him—

"He is lying in his bed, and he is seik and sair,

Let him lye in till that bedd monthes two and dayes thrie mair!

He sall lye in till his bed, he salbe seik and sair,

He sall lye in till his bedd, monthes two and dayes thrie mair!"

When they said these words they were all on their knees with their hair about their shoulders and eyes, holding up their hands to the devil, beseeching him to destroy Mr Harry; and then it was decided to go into his chamber and swing the bag over him. Bessie Hay—Able-and-Stout—undertook this office, and she went to his room, being intimate with him, the bag in her hands and her mind set on slaying him by its means; but there were some worthy persons with him at the time, so Bessie did no harm, only swung a few drops on him which did not kill him. They had a hard taskmaster in the devil—Black Johnnie, as they used to call him among themselves. But he used to overhear them, and would suddenly appear in the midst of them, saying, "I ken weill anewgh what ye wer saying of me," and then would beat and buffet them sore. He was always beating them, specially if they were absent from any of the meetings, or if they forgot anything he had told them to do. Alexander Elder was being continually thrashed. He was very soft and could never defend himself in the least, but would cry and scream when the devil scourged him. The women had more pluck. Margaret Wilson—Pickle-nearest-the-wind—would defend herself finely, throwing up her hands to keep the strokes from her; and Bessie Wilson—Throw-the-corn-yard—"would speak crusty with her tongue and would be belling against him soundly." He used to beat them all up and down with scourges and sharp cords, they like naked ghosts crying, "Pity! pity! mercy! mercy, our Lord!" But he would have neither pity nor mercy, but would grin at them like a dog, and as if he would swallow them up. He would give them most beautiful money, at least to look at; but in four-and-twenty hours it would be all gone, or changed to mere dirt and rubbish. The devil wore sometimes boots and sometimes shoes, but ever his feet were cloven, and ever his colour black. This, with some small variations, was the sum of what Isobell Gowdie confessed in her four depositions taken between the 13th of April and 27th of May in the year of grace 1662.

Janet Braidhead, spouse to John Taylor, followed next. Her first confession, made on the 14th of April, set forth how that she had known nothing of witchcraft until her husband and his mother, Elspeth Nishie, had taught her; her first lesson from them being the making of some "drugs" which were to charm away the fruit and corn, and kill the cattle, of one John Hay in the Mure. After that, she was taken to the kirk at Auldearne, where her husband presented her for the devil's baptism and marking, which were done in the usual manner. She also gave evidence of the clay picture which was to destroy all the male children of the Laird of Park; and she gave a long list of the frequenters of the Sabbaths, including some of the most respectable inhabitants of the place; and in many other things she confirmed Isobell Gowdie's depositions, specially in all regarding the devil and the unequivocal nature of their connection with him, which was put into plain and unmistakable language enough.

We are not told the ultimate fate of Isobell Gowdie and Janet Braidhead, but they had confessed enough to burn half Scotland, and it is not likely that they escaped the doom assigned to their order.

WITCH SPIRITS

Year by year witches became scarcer, none of any special note presenting themselves till we come to the case of Margaret Nin-Gilbert, of Caithness, which happened in the year 1718; the same year as that in which the minister of Redcastle lost his life by witchcraft, and Mr M'Gill's house at Kinross (he was minister there) was so egregiously troubled by a spirit which nipped the sheets and stuck pins into eggs and meat, and clipt away the laps of a gentlewoman's hood and a servant maid's gown tail, and flung stones down the chimney, which "wambled a space" on the floor, and then took a flight out of the window, and threw the minister's bible into the fire, and spoilt the baking, and played all sorts of mad pranks to disquiet the family and defy God. If such things as these could be done in the light of the sun, why, should not Margaret Nin-Gilbert have supernatural power? Nin-Gilbert had a friend, one Maragret Olson, a woman of it is said wicked behaviour, whom Mr Frazer put out of her house, taking as his tenant instead one William Montgomerie. Upon this Margaret Olson went to her friend Nin-Gilbert, the notorious witch, and besought her to harm Mr Frazer; but Mr Frazer being a gentleman of rank and fortune was defended from the witches, and Nin-Gilbert confessed she had no power or inclination to hurt him. However, one night as he was crossing a bridge, they attempted him, but succeeded not; and he, on being questioned, said he perfectly remembered "his horse making a great adoe at that place, but that by the Lord's goodness he escaped." Also he had a gteat sickness at that time these women were taken, but he had common sense enough to refuse to ascribe it to them. Finding that they could not prevail against Mr Frazer, they turned their attention to Montgomerie, "mason, in Burnside of Scrabster," who was also under the ban for having accepted the tenancy of which Margaret Olson had been dispossessed. Suddenly his house became so infested with cats that it was no longer safe for his family to remain there. He himself was away, but his wife sent to him five times, threatening that if he did not return home to protect them, she would flit to Thurso; and his servant left them suddenly, and in mid term, because five of these cats came one night to the fireside where she was alone, and began speaking among themselves with human and intelligible voices. So William Montgomerie, mason at Scrabster, returned home to do battle with the enemy. The cats came in their old way and in their old numbers; and William prepared his best. On Friday night, the 28th of November, one of the cats got into a chest with a hole in it, and when she put her head out of the hole, William made a lunge at her with his sword, which "cutt hir," but for all that he could not hold her. He then opened the chest, and his servant, William Geddes, stuck his dirk into her hind quarters and pinned her to the chest. After which, Montgomerie beat her with his sword and cast her out for dead; but the next morning she was gone; so there was no doubt as to her true character. Four or five nights after this, his servant, being in bed, "cryed out that Some of these catts had come in on him." Montgomerie ran to his aid, wrapt his plaid about the cat and thrust his dirk through her body, then smashed her head with the back of an axe, and cast her out like the first. The next morning she too was gone, and there was proof positive for another case. So as none of these cats belonged to the neighbourhood, and there were eight of them assembled together in one night, "this looking like witchcraft, it being threatened that none should thrive in my said house," William Montgomerie made petition to the Sheriff-Depute of Caithness, to visit "some person of bad fame," who was reported to have fallen sick immediately on this encounter, and search out if she had any wounds on her body or not. "This representation seeming all the time to be very incredulous and fabulous, the sheriff had no manner of regard yrto." But when, on the 12th of February, Margaret Nin-Gilbert was seen by one of her neighbours "to drop at her own door one of her leggs from the midle, and she, being under bad fame for witchcraft, the legg, black and putrified, was brought before the Sheriff-Depute" (not the sheriff himself, the Earl of Caithness, who might have had a little more common sense)—then the said Sheriff-Depute ordered Nin-Gilbert to be seized and examined. Margaret made short work of it. Being interrogated the 8th of February, 1719, she confessed that she was under compact with the devil, whom she had met in the likeness of a black man as she was travelling some long time byegone in ane evening; confessed also that he sometimes appeared to her as a great black horse, and other times as if riding on a black horse, and sometimes as a black cloud, and sometimes as a black hen. Confessed also that she was at William Montgomerie's house that evening, when he attacked her as a cat, and that he broke her leg with the dirk or axe, which since had fallen off from the rest of her body: also, that Margaret Olson was there with her, who, being stronger than she did cast her on the dirk when her leg was broken. She then delated four other women, one of whom Helen Andrew, had been so crushed and maimed by Montgomerie, "that she dyed that same night of her wounds or few days yrafter:" and another, M'Huistan, "cast herself a few days afterwards from the rocks of Borrowstoun into the sea, since which time she was never seen;" while a third, Jannet Pyper, she identified as having a red petticoat on her. Asked how they managed not be be discovered said, "the devil raised a fog or mist to conceal them." When her confession was ended, her accomplices were apprehended; but she herself died in prison in a fortnight's time. Margaret Olson was then examined. She was "tryed in the shoulders" (for witches' marks), "where there were several small spots, some read, some blewish; after a needle was driven in with great force almost to the eye she felt it not. Mr. Innes, Mr Oswald, minister, and several honest women, and Bailzie Forbes, were witnesses to this. And further, that while the needle was in her shoulder, as aforesaid, she said, 'Am not I ane honest woman now?'" So this instance of human wickedness and folly ended by the usual method of the cord and the stake.

THE LAST OF THE WITCHES

And now we draw near to the close of this fatal superstition. In 1726, Woodrow notes "some pretty odd accounts of witches," had from a couple of Ross-shire men, but fails to give us very accurate details, save only that one of them at her death "confessed that they had, by sorcery, taken away the sight of one of the eyes of an Episcopal minister, who lost the sight of his eye upon a sudden, and could give no reason for it." And early in the year of 1727 the last witch-fire was kindled with which the air of bonnie Scotland was polluted. Two poor Highland women, a mother and daughter, were brought before Captain David Ross of Littledean, deputy-sheriff of Sutherland, charged with witchcraft and consorting with the devil. The mother was accused of having used her daughter as her "horse and hattock," causing her to be shod by the devil, so that she was ever after lame in both hands and feet; and the fact being satisfactorily proved, and Captain David Ross being well assured of the same, the poor old woman was put into a tar-barrel and burned at Dornoch in the bright month of June. "And it is said that after being brought out to execution, the weather proving very severe, she sat composedly warming herself by the fire prepared to consume her, while the other instruments of death were getting ready." The daughter escaped: afterwards she married and had a son who was as lame as herself; and lame in the same manner too; though it does not seem that he was ever shod by the devil and witch-ridden. "And this son," says Sir Walter Scott, in 1830, "was living so lately as to receive the charity of the present Marchioness of Stafford, Countess of Sutherland in her own right."

This, then, is the last execution for witchcraft in Scotland; and in June, 1736, the Acts Anentis Witchcraft were formally repealed. Henceforth, to the dread of the timid, and the anger of the pious, the English Parliament distinctly opposed the express letter of the Law of God, "Thou shalt not suffer a witch to live;" and declared the text upon which so much critical absurdity had been talked, and in support of which so much innocent blood had been shed, vain, superstitious, impossible, and contrary to that human reason which is the highest law of God hitherto revealed unto men. But if Parliament could stay executions it could not remove beliefs, nor give rationality in place of folly. Not more than sixty years ago an old woman named Elizabeth M'Whirter was "scratched" by one Eaglesham, in the parish of Colmonel, Ayrshire, because his son had fallen sick, and the neighbours said he was betwitched. Poor old Bessie M'Whirter was forced over the hills to the young man's house, a distance of three miles, and there made to kneel by his bedside and repeat the Lord's Prayer. When she had finished, the youth's father took a rusty nail and scratched the poor old creature's brow in the form of a cross; scratched it so effectually that it was many weeks in healing, and the scar remained to the last day of her life. If Elizabeth M'Whirter had lived a generation earlier, she might have run a race with death and a tar barrel, and been defeated at the end, like the poor old wretch at Dornoch.

But still the old faith lingers in those beautiful vales, and hides in the fastnesses of the mountain glens; still brownies haunt the ruined places, and witches send forth blight and bale at their will; still the elfin people ride on the whirlwind and dance in the moonlight; and the hill and the flood and the brae and the streamlet have their attendant spirits which vie with the churchyard ghost in impotent malevolence to men. And the gift of second sight, though dying out because of these degenerate times of utilitarianism and power-loom weaving, is yet to be found where the old blood runs thickest, and the old ideas are least disturbed; and still the whole nation clings with spasmodic force to its gloomy creed of the Predestined and the Elect, and holds by the early faith from whose narrow bounds others have emerged into a brighter and wider path. No more witch-fires are now lighted on the Castle Hill; no more grave and reverend divines give themselves up, like Mr John Aird, to discovering the devil's mark stamped visibly on human flesh; yet the heart of the people has not abandoned its ancient God, and though the altars may be dressed with the flowers of another season, and the name upon the plinth be carved in other characters, yet is the indwelling idol the same. The God which Calvinistic Scotland yet worships is the same God as that to which the witches and wizards of old were sacrificed; he is the God of Superstition, the God of Condemnation, in whose temple Nature has no place, and Humanity no rights.

*Loathsome.

*Spells.

*Twisted or wrenched.

*Shield from evil influence.

+To go about under the influence of strong passion.

*To the outer room.

+To the inner room.

*A common type of country bread made with water.

*On life: alive.

CPSIA information can be obtained
at www.ICGtesting.com
Printed in the USA
BVHW071704271222
655066BV00019B/209